Reading for TODAY

Workbook Six

PROGRAM AUTHORS

Linda Ward Beech • **Tara McCarthy**

PROGRAM CONSULTANTS

Myra K. Baum
Office of Adult and
   Continuing Education
Brooklyn, New York

Francis J. Feltman, Jr.
Racine Youth Offender
   Correctional Facility
Racine, Wisconsin

Mary Ann Guilliams
Gary Job Corps
San Marcos, Texas

Julie Jacobs
Inmate Literacy Project
Santa Clara County Library
Milpitas, California

Maxine L. McCormick
Workforce Education
Orange County Public Schools
Orlando, Florida

Sandra S. Owens
Laurens County Literacy Council
Laurens, South Carolina

STECK-VAUGHN
ELEMENTARY · SECONDARY · ADULT · LIBRARY

A Harcourt Company

www.steck-vaughn.com

Acknowledgments

STAFF CREDITS

Executive Editor: Ellen Northcutt

Senior Editor: Donna Townsend

Supervising Designer: Pamela Heaney

Designer: Jessica Bristow

ILLUSTRATION CREDITS: Holly Cooper, Joan Pilch

ISBN 0-7398-2958-0

Printed in the United States of America

1 2 3 4 5 6 7 8 9 10 RP 04 03 02 01 00

Contents

To the Instructor

The *Reading for Today* workbooks are designed to accompany the new structure of the *Reading for Today* student books. Books 1–6 have corresponding workbooks that follow the same format in:

- controlled vocabulary
- reading level
- phonics and word-building skills
- sight vocabulary
- writing and comprehension skills

Student Book ➡	Workbook
UNIT CONTENTS	**UNIT CONTENTS**
• Discussion	• Discussion
• Sight words/vocabulary	• Reading practice
• Phonics/word study skills	• Phonics/word study generalizations
• Writing skills	• Writing applications
• Reading selection	• Extended reading selection
• Comprehension questions	• Comprehension questions
• Life-coping skills	• Writing practice

The chart shows how a typical unit in a *Reading for Today* workbook serves as a follow-up for its corresponding unit in a *Reading for Today* student book.

Students who use the *Reading for Today* workbooks, however, do not simply review, practice, and reinforce sight words, phonics, and writing skills. Students also extend their learning. They read additional adult-related stories that are written with the controlled vocabulary that puts the reading within their grasp. Learners discuss what they bring of their own experience to the reading selections by responding to purpose-setting questions, thus sharpening their thinking and discussion skills. And learners write, both to demonstrate comprehension and to respond in their own way to the reading selections.

Teaching Suggestions

Each unit in the *Reading for Today* Workbook Six follows the pattern outlined below.

Reading and Discussing   Pages 3 and 4

Objectives: To help the student see the connection between reading and speaking. To improve comprehension through discussion.

Teaching Steps:

A. Read the question or questions. Encourage the student to talk about the question. Discussing the question will help the student get ready to read the story that follows.

B. Help the student read the story. Remember to praise the student's efforts.

C. Talk about the story. Help the student answer the discussion question that follows the story. Reread the story if necessary.

Vocabulary   Pages 5 and 6

Objective: To review the words introduced in previous units. To practice a specific vocabulary skill.

Teaching Steps: Be sure the student understands the directions for each exercise. Have students check their answers by referring to the Answer Key at the back of the book.

Reading Practice   Page 7

Objective: To practice reading word groups or phrases rather than individual words.

Teaching Steps:

A. Help the student read and reread each phrase until each one is smooth and natural. Praise the student's success.

B. Help the student fill in the blanks correctly.

C. Practice reading the entire story for fluency. Rereading the story after practicing the phrasing will give the student a sense of success.

Writing Skills   Page 8

Objective: To review and reinforce the writing skill taught in the student book.

Teaching Steps: Help the student understand the directions for each exercise. Have students check their answers by referring to the Answer Key at the back of the book.

Comprehension   Pages 9, 10, and 11

Objectives: To read the conclusion of the story and answer comprehension questions in writing. To review a specific comprehension skill introduced in the corresponding student book unit.

Teaching Steps:

A. Have the student read the story.

B. Have the student write the answers to the questions. The following hints will help the learner succeed.

  1. The answer to the question may often be found stated directly in the story.

  2. Rereading the story after reading a question may make it easier to answer the question.

  3. Some questions can be answered by turning the question into a statement and completing the statement with the answer from the story.

C. Have the student review the specific comprehension skill in the corresponding student book unit. Be sure the student understands the directions for the exercise. Have students check their answers by referring to the Answer Key at the back of the book.

From Reading to Writing   Page 12

Objectives: To give students an opportunity to write about their own lives or life experiences. To reinforce reading by writing something for someone else to read.

Teaching Steps:

A. Encourage the student to get as many ideas or thoughts on paper as possible. Praise any legitimate attempts to write. Try for more clarity only as your student gains confidence in writing.

B. When your student finishes writing, you may wish to go back over the writing and follow the suggestions in Part B of each writing page.

READING AND DISCUSSING

A. Discuss.

How can a play be a powerful form of communication?

B. Read the story.

The Power of a Play

In 1965 a young man bought a typewriter for twenty dollars. Neither the young man nor the world of drama would ever be the same. The young man was August Wilson. The typewriter was the start of his career as a writer. Although Wilson began as a poet, he is known as a playwright today. The plays that he writes are about the African-American experience.

Wilson's major project is to write a cycle of ten plays. Each play is about a decade of the twentieth century and an issue faced by African Americans during that time. He explores the choices they have made and the directions they have taken. His goal is to show the importance of tradition and culture to African-American people. Wilson's plays have won many big awards. Perhaps the most important recognition has come from the audiences who see his work. They have gone to see his plays in the famous Broadway theaters of New York City and in other cities across the country.

Writing from Experience

August Wilson was born in 1945 in Pittsburgh, Pennsylvania. His mother was African American and his father was white. Wilson was one of six children who grew up in a two-room apartment. His father, a baker, did not spend much time with the family. The Wilsons were poor and often struggled to get by.

Young August learned to read when he was four. He remembers being curious about words, their meaning, their sounds, and how they are formed. Even so, August did not stay in school past the age of 15. As an African-American student in a mostly white school, he was often teased. The final blow came when he wrote a paper on Napoleon. He was accused of cheating because the paper was so good.

Although he dropped out of school, Wilson went right on reading. At the public library he read the books of African-American writers such as Langston Hughes, Richard Wright, and Ralph Ellison. He also read poetry by Imanu Amiri Baraka, Dylan Thomas, and many other poets.

Wilson learned to be a good observer during this time. He watched how people behaved. He listened to them talk. He heard the pattern of their speech and the choice of their words. He noticed, too, the places where people gathered to talk—the street corners, front porches, even the local barbershop. Years later these things served Wilson well as he created characters and settings for his plays. For example, the barbershop in *Ma Rainey's Black Bottom* is a meeting place for men. It is also a place where ideas are expressed. Much of the action in his play *Fences* happens in the yard and on the porch of the family's home. Another play, *Two Trains Running*, is set in a restaurant. Almost all of Wilson's plays take place in his old neighborhood in the city of Pittsburgh.

From Poet to Playwright

The first thing Wilson typed on his typewriter in 1965 was his name. He wanted "to see how it looked in print." Then he typed his poems. Over the next few years, some of these poems were published in small magazines. Wilson also became involved in the "Black Power" movement of the late 60s and early 70s. The aim of this movement was to give African Americans more rights and a bigger voice. During this time, Wilson started a theater company to express the African-American point of view. Some of his first plays were produced there.

In 1978 Wilson went to St. Paul, Minnesota, where he visited a friend who was the director of a theater. While in St. Paul, Wilson wrote *Jitney*, the first play in his ten-play cycle. This drama, set in a Pittsburgh gypsy-cab station, is about the struggle of several African-American taxi drivers in the 1970s.

C. Think About It

What experiences from your life would you include in a play? What have you observed that you could write about?

audience	commitment	culture	passionate	reminisce
relative	recognition	influence	creative	published

A. Choose the correct word to complete each sentence.

1. (relatives, audiences) Wilson's plays appeal to _____ of many backgrounds.

2. (passionate, recognition) Many of the _____ speeches by Wilson's characters come from his growing-up years.

3. (reminisced, influenced) The poets and writers that Wilson read have also _____ him.

4. (commitment, culture) Wilson has a deep _____ to his work.

5. (creative, published) August Wilson's plays have been _____ in book form, too.

B. Read the clues. Choose words from the word box to complete the puzzle.

Across

1. new and original
3. printed for the public
4. with great feeling
7. pledge or promise
8. having an effect on
9. fame

Down

2. family member
5. viewers
6. recall
7. art and tradition of a group

 **Multiple Meanings**

Each word in dark type below has more than one meaning. Read the meanings and the sentences. Write the letter of the meaning that best fits the way the word is used in the sentence.

The word *sharp* can mean:

a. having a cutting edge or fine point
b. involving a quick change in direction
c. harsh or critical
d. above the correct pitch in music
e. quick to understand

_____ **1.** The band played a sharp note.

_____ **2.** The character in the play has a sharp knife.

_____ **3.** Drama critics sometimes have sharp words for playwrights.

_____ **4.** Although August Wilson was sharp, he did not stay in school.

_____ **5.** Make a sharp right to find your seats in the theater.

The word *border* can mean:

a. the edge of an area
b. a line that separates countries or states
c. a design around the edge of something
d. to be close to

_____ **6.** Do Wilson's plays border on being a story of his life?

_____ **7.** The piano had a carved border along the top.

_____ **8.** When you go from the South to Pennsylvania, you cross several state borders.

_____ **9.** The fence formed a border between yards.

Reading Practice

A. Read the phrases in the box aloud. Practice until you can read them smoothly.

> 1. has won great recognition
> 2. passionate men and women
> 3. When asked about influences
> 4. the creative force
> 5. represents African-American culture
> 6. Wilson's commitment
> 7. While thinking back
> 8. For audiences

B. Write the phrases to complete the paragraph.

August Wilson _____
                            1

for his fine plays. Most of his characters are _____
                                                       2

_____ trying to come to terms with life.

_____
            3

on his work, Wilson has often mentioned _____
                                                 4

_____ of the blues. He feels this music truly

_____ .
            5

Indeed, _____ to this music led to
                    6

his play, *Ma Rainey's Black Bottom.* _____
                                             7

_____ about the origins of this play, he has recalled

buying a Ma (Gertrude) Rainey album in 1978. _____
                                                      8

_____ unfamiliar with the play, the title refers to a

dance popular in the 1920s when the story takes place.

C. Read the paragraph aloud. Practice until you can read it smoothly.

Review what you have learned about adjectives on page 16 of *Reading for Today Book Six*. Then complete the exercises below.

A. Read each sentence and circle the adjective.

1. To turn a memory into a play is a creative act.

2. August Wilson has a passionate interest in the blues.

3. He likes the music of the famous Bessie Smith.

4. He says this is an important influence on his work.

5. Wilson's plays tell powerful stories on stage.

6. He has been praised for his humor and lively language.

B. In each sentence below, fill in the blanks using the adjective that fits in the sentence.

1. (interesting, interest) A playwright has to create

   _____ characters.

2. (believe, believable) The actors must be _____
   to bring the play alive.

3. (careful, carefully) A _____ director tries to get
   the playwright's words across.

4. (those, exciting) Opening night is _____ for
   everyone involved.

5. (big, very) Will the play be a _____ hit?

C. Write sentences of your own using each of the adjectives below.

1. wonderful _____

   _____

2. seven _____

   _____

3. spicy _____

   _____

Comprehension

A. Read the story to find out more about August Wilson.

The Power of a Play

Wilson's big break came in 1981. That year he sent his play *Ma Rainey's Black Bottom* to a national playwrights' group. Wilson's play was chosen to be read aloud for the group's annual meeting. This was a big step. It made Wilson really begin to think of himself as a playwright. He also found that the comments of other writers were very helpful. He found that a play can grow and change as the author shapes and reshapes it. Wilson now says that creating a play is like putting together a collage (a kind of picture made from different objects or shapes put together). The parts of the collage are the characters, the setting, the plot, and the dialog. Only when these parts come together, does the play make sense.

Thinking About Fences

Wilson's next play was called *Fences*. The story is about a family in the 1950s, but it is also about the family's past when their relatives were slaves. The youngest members of the family have hopes for better lives, but their father, Troy, doesn't share their hope. Troy feels that he has never really had an equal chance even though he has been willing to work hard. As a young man, Troy had been a very good baseball player, but opportunities for African-American players were limited then. So, when Troy's son wants to play ball, Troy opposes him. Is it jealousy? Or is he trying to protect his son from the disappointment he knew?

The title for the play *Fences* comes from the fence that Troy is building around his yard. Is it to keep people, things, and events in or to keep them out? Like the characters in the play, the audience must try to decide.

Ghosts of the Past

After *Fences* Wilson wrote *Joe Turner's Come and Gone*. In this play set in 1911, Herald Loomis and his daughter have moved from the South to a boarding house in Pittsburgh. Herald has just spent seven years of forced labor working on a chain gang for Joe Turner. As the title suggests, Joe Turner has come and gone in Herald's life, but the damage remains. Herald's spirit is broken. He hopes he can find the wife he lost touch with and get back his old self.

Another Wilson play, *The Piano Lesson*, is set in the 1930s. Boy Willie and his sister Berniece disagree on the fate of a piano that has been in their family for more than 130 years. At one time it had been used to buy freedom for members of their family. In the play Boy Willie is battling the ghost of Sutter, a slave master from the past. Boy Willie wants to sell the piano and use the money to buy land from Sutter's relatives. Berniece wants the piano to stay in the family. In their own ways the characters must work out their feelings about the piano and about the past.

August Wilson says he got the idea for the title of this play from a painting with the same name. The painting is by a well-known African-American artist, Romare Bearden. Wilson admires Bearden for the way he portrays African-American life. Wilson feels that African Americans don't have enough good symbols of the past. He thinks they need to connect more to the culture and traditions that kept them going in the past. As his plays show, this is not always easy when you are trying to survive the present and step into the future, too. But Wilson doesn't stop there. He feels that this conflict is true for all cultures. That is what audiences see and feel, too. And that is what makes his plays so moving.

B. Answer the questions using complete sentences.

1. What are the people and places in a play called?

   _____

   _____

2. Where do most of Wilson's plays take place?

   _____

   _____

3. What is the title of one of Wilson's plays?

   _____

   _____

4. What conflict does Wilson feel is true for all cultures?

   _____

   _____

   _____

Character Traits

On page 14 of *Reading for Today Book Six*, you learned the steps for recognizing character traits. Review those steps before practicing the skill here.

A. Read the paragraphs. Fill in the circle for the traits that best describe the character.

Jack walked along in the sunshine, whistling a slightly off-key tune. He tipped his hat to a woman pushing a baby carriage and stopped to dig in his pocket for a dollar to give the man jiggling a cup on the corner. Walking had made him a few minutes late for work, but Jack never let things like that bother him.

1. Jack is

○ **a.** lazy
○ **b.** generous
○ **c.** happy-go-lucky
○ **d.** shy

Miranda picked up the phone to make another call. Speaking in hushed, excited tones she told her friend Doreen all about the scandal of Cousin Otis. This was the third time she had repeated the tale that morning. Each time she added more details to the story.

2. Miranda is

○ **a.** dramatic
○ **b.** a gossip
○ **c.** thoughtful
○ **d.** afraid

B. Write a paragraph that shows a character trait of someone you know.

_____

_____

_____

_____

_____

_____

A. August Wilson says that he often starts a play with a line of dialog. In this way he gets to know his characters. Think about some lines of dialog that appeal to you. Write them down. Then think about a character who would say them. Write a paragraph describing that character. You might want to use some of the words and phrases in the box below.

Words	Phrases
relatives	represent a culture
passionate	reminisce about the past
influences	from one generation to another
portrait	searching for an identity

_____

_____

_____

_____

_____

_____

_____

_____

_____

_____

_____

_____

B. Read your paragraph. Have you described a character with specific traits? Are there examples to support what the character might say and how the character might act? Make any changes that you think are needed.

READING AND DISCUSSING

A. Discuss.

What technology skills do workers need these days? How do you feel when you're faced with new ways of doing things?

B. Read the story.

Old Skills and New Skills

Carmen's old friends from school met as often as they could at the Bumble Bee Inn restaurant. It was always great to remember good times together and to talk about what was new in each other's lives. But until lately, nothing had been really new for Carmen. For years and years, she had just been taking care of her kids and doing odd jobs to keep some money coming in. But Carmen knew that things were different now. All the kids were grown up and on their own. Carmen wanted to get back into the swing of things with a full-time job.

At the Bumble Bee Inn one evening, Carmen told her friends about wanting full-time employment. Right away, it seemed like everyone had an idea or a suggestion.

"As I remember," said Rudy, "in school, you were pretty savvy about music. You were a fine piano player, and you knew all the hit songs, all the musicians, all the latest records and tapes. If you're still an up-to-date music fan, Carmen, I may have a spot for you at Sam's Sound Store. I'm the assistant manager there now."

"Hey!" said Al, "Don't forget Ridge Market! I've got an opening there right now in the produce department. I remember how quick you are to catch on to numbers and procedures, Carmen. Stop in and see me about it."

Elsa jumped in with an idea of her own. "Carmen," she said, "I always thought your real strength was in dealing with people. You might like working with me at the reception desk at the Sleepy Hollow Motel. The woman who worked there with me has just retired. Come around and see what the job involves."

All of a sudden, it seemed to Carmen like she had more opportunities than she could handle!

The next morning, Carmen set out to explore the jobs her friends had suggested. At Ridge Market, her first stop, Al greeted her with his usual big smile and cheery hello. On a tour of the market, he explained the various scanning wands and pricing guns that a produce manager had to know about. Carmen nodded and smiled. It sounded like a job she could learn to do pretty quickly.

But at the end of the tour, she said to Al, "You know, old friend, you're great to show me around, but I just don't know yet if this is the job for me. With four kids to buy food for, I feel like I've already spent most of my life in a grocery store."

Carmen continued with her job search. Her next stop was at Rudy's music store. "I hope you can spend a couple of hours here," said Rudy. "I have a lot to show you." And indeed he did! Carmen was amazed to find out about the technology that was helping musicians, singers, and music lovers of all kinds work in ways she had never imagined.

For example, one of Rudy's customers was a woman named Tanya. Tanya said, "I got a call from California last night. My boss there needs a new song for his ad by this morning. I wrote the music out, but I don't know how to get it out to California so fast."

"No problem, Tanya," said Rudy. "Did you bring the music chart with you? Do you have your boss's e-mail address?"

"I sure do," said Tanya.

"Then let's get to work," said Rudy. He sat down at a synthesizer keyboard and played Tanya's song a couple of times. Then he had it just right.

"That's perfect!" said Tanya.

"OK," said Rudy. "I'll do the final run." As he played the song again, he ran it through something called a MIDI and then pushed it into e-mail. "Your boss will have this song in a few minutes," he said to Tanya. Tanya left with a smile on her face.

"I'm not sure how that worked," said Carmen to Rudy.

"Doesn't matter," said Rudy. "You'll learn fast. When do you want to start?"

C. Think about it.

Do you think Carmen will take the job at the music store? Explain why or why not. What might influence her decision?

Vocabulary   Review

productive	reliable	ambition	requirements	accuracy
circulars	convenient	frequently	inventory	access

A. Choose the correct word to complete each sentence.

1. (ambition, accuracy) Carmen's _____ was to get a full-time job.

2. (requirements, reliable) Rudy thought Carmen would be a _____ worker.

3. (inventory, access) Rudy has _____ to computers and the Internet.

4. (productive, convenient) Carmen wants to be a _____ worker.

B. Read the clues. Choose words from the word box to complete the puzzle.

frequently	edge	productive	inventory	accuracy	live
access	star	circulars	stay	sick	

Across

3. creating a lot
6. be alive; reside
8. a heavenly body; an actor or singer
9. mailed ads or notices
10. remain

Down

1. often
2. border or margin
4. a complete list of articles
5. correctness
7. a right to use or approach
8. ill

A. Match the words with their meanings. Write the letter. (The stressed syllable is underlined.)

_____	1. <u>con</u>tent	**a.**	trash
_____	2. <u>pro</u>duce	**b.**	dry, sandy region
_____	3. <u>de</u>sert	**c.**	give an opposing opinion
_____	4. <u>ob</u>ject	**d.**	what is inside
_____	5. <u>re</u>fuse	**e.**	make something
_____	6. re<u>fuse</u>	**f.**	leave alone
_____	7. con<u>tent</u>	**g.**	say no; won't do
_____	8. pro<u>duce</u>	**h.**	an item
_____	9. ob<u>ject</u>	**i.**	happy; satisfied
_____	10. de<u>sert</u>	**j.**	farm products

B. Read each sentence. Circle the syllable to stress in each underlined word. Then write the letter from A to show which meaning is used in the sentence.

_____	1. Carmen's friends won't <u>desert</u> her.
_____	2. She's not <u>content</u> to stay home.
_____	3. Her kids don't <u>object</u> to her working.
_____	4. She'd like to <u>produce</u> a good income.
_____	5. The job market was like a <u>desert</u>.
_____	6. Carmen read the <u>contents</u> of the help-wanted page.
_____	7. She won't <u>refuse</u> an interesting job.
_____	8. Al offered her one in the <u>produce</u> department.

A. Read the phrases aloud. Practice until you can read them smoothly.

> 1. frequently read
> 2. a productive and reliable worker
> 3. Another of Carmen's ambitions
> 4. one of Carmen's requirements
> 5. keeping an inventory
> 6. circulars for customers

B. Write the phrases to complete the paragraph.

Carmen _____ 1 _____ the help-wanted ads. She knew she would be _____ 2 _____

_____ if she found the right job.

_____ 3 _____ was to start her own business some day. So, _____ 4 _____

_____ was a job where she could learn about

_____ 5 _____ and writing

_____ 6 _____.

C. Read the paragraph aloud. Practice until you can read it smoothly.

Writing Names and Titles

Review what you have learned about capitalizing names and titles on page 34 of *Reading for Today Book Six*. Then complete the exercises below.

A. **Decide which of the words in the box should be capitalized. Write those words correctly on the lines.**

angela's cafe	los angeles, california
the garden show	ms. linda torez
new year's day	kent city journal

_____

_____

_____

_____

_____

_____

B. **Rewrite each sentence using capital letters correctly.**

1. Carmen moved from pen street to a larger apartment on worth avenue. _____

    _____

2. The new apartment was near fairfield community college and jiffy food mart. _____

    _____

3. On saturdays and sundays, carmen walked to the park with floyd and maria. _____

    _____

A. Continue reading the story about Carmen's search for a job.

Old Skills and New Skills

Rudy's next customer was a singer named Fred. Fred said, "I need some back-up for this song I sang by myself." He handed a tape to Rudy.

"No problem!" said Rudy. He put on the tape, threw some switches, and before long Fred had a new tape with a back-up bass and guitar. Fred looked very pleased as he left the store.

Carmen said, " I don't think Fred is a very good singer. But you sure made him sound better with the back-up!"

"That's business!" said Rudy. "So, like I said, are you ready to start working here?"

"I have to visit Rita before I make up my mind," said Carmen. "Thanks for the tour and the offer, Rudy. I'll get back to you real soon."

"Yeah, well, we're all meeting again at the Bumble Bee Inn tonight," said Rudy. "You can let me know your decision then."

Two More Stops

Carmen was quite impressed by the Sleepy Hollow Motel and by the way Elsa handled her work there. As Carmen walked in, Elsa was just hanging up the phone.

"Some of these customers present problems," said Elsa. "For example, that was a woman who wanted to reserve a room for tonight and tomorrow night that overlooked the swimming pool. I checked the reservation list on the computer and I could see that we had no such room available for tonight. However, we do have one for tomorrow, and I was able to convince the woman to take an alternate room for tonight."

"How did you convince her?" asked Carmen.

"Once again, I looked at the guest list on the computer," said Elsa. "I could see that this woman and her family have stayed here a lot before. Because she's a good customer, I could offer her a special reduced rate on the rooms. She went for it and seemed really happy."

The phone rang again and again, and at the same time several people stood in line to check in or out of the Sleepy Hollow. When things had quieted down a bit, Elsa said, "Well, you can see that we need another full-time person here to help me out! How about it, Carmen?"

"Let me think about it" said Carmen. "I've got so many possible jobs! I'm grateful for that because I know that's not the way it usually is, but I want to turn things over in my mind before I decide."

As she rode the bus home, Carmen glanced up and saw a sign she had passed many times before: *Nancy's Nursery*. "That's what I need for a change of pace," thought Carmen. "I'll buy myself a pot of tulips, put them on my windowsill at home, and give this job hunting a rest for a couple of hours!"

Carmen pulled the stop cord, got off the bus, and wandered into Nancy's. The place was alive with the wonderful scents of flowering plants, an aroma that had always made Carmen feel cheerful and energetic. And posted right by the doors was a sign that said *Help Wanted: Full-time position open. Applicant must enjoy outdoor work. Great opportunity to learn all about the gardening business!*

A woman with a lapel pin that said *Nancy* walked up to Carmen. "May I help you?" she asked.

"I think so!" said Carmen. "Maybe I can help you, too!"

At the Bumble Bee Inn that evening, Carmen announced to her friends that she had finally found the job she wanted. "It's at a nursery," she said.

"A nursery!" her friends all said at once.

Elsa said, "I thought you were tired of taking care of kids!"

"Not *that* kind of nursery!" laughed Carmen. She explained what her new job was.

"Sounds like hard work," said Rudy. "Like old-fashioned, down-on-your-knees hard work!"

"Don't worry, Rudy," said Carmen. "Nancy has a whole computerized ordering system set up inside her nursery. I'll be learning that as well as the old-fashioned hard work!"

B. Write a complete sentence to answer each question.

1. What kind of job did Elsa offer Carmen? _____

_____

2. Do you think Carmen's friends were surprised at the job she chose?

   Explain why you think so. _____

_____

3. Why do you think Carmen chose to work at a nursery? _____

_____

Comprehension — Cause and Effect

A. Each phrase states an effect. Decide if answer *a*, *b*, or *c* is the cause. Fill in the circle beside the best answer

1. Carmen was ready for a full-time job

   ○ **a.** because her kids were now on their own.
   ○ **b.** even though she wasn't sure what kind of job she wanted.
   ○ **c.** that would give her a steady income.

2. Carmen's friends would help her

   ○ **a.** and give her some encouragement.
   ○ **b.** with ideas and suggestions.
   ○ **c.** if she came to visit their workplaces.

3. Carmen took the job at the nursery

   ○ **a.** that she stopped at on her way home.
   ○ **b.** because she liked plants.
   ○ **c.** and told her friends why she did it.

B. Each phrase states a cause. Decide if answer *a*, *b*, or *c* is the effect. Fill in the circle beside the best answer.

1. Rudy knew that Carmen was good in music

   ○ **a.** when she was in school years ago.
   ○ **b.** and that she could play the piano.
   ○ **c.** so he offered her a job at his store.

2. The job at the music store didn't interest Carmen,

   ○ **a.** so she went on to Elsa's workplace.
   ○ **b.** any more than the one at Al's store.
   ○ **c.** even though she could do the work.

3. Nancy needed an outdoor helper

   ○ **a.** because her business was booming.
   ○ **b.** and, as a result, she hired Carmen.
   ○ **c.** and Carmen liked outdoor work.

From Reading to Writing

A. What kind of job would <u>your</u> ideal job be? Why would you like that job? Write a paragraph about the job-of-your-dreams. You may want to use some of the phrases below.

my greatest ambition	full-time or part-time work
meet the job requirements	a chance to get ahead in the world
a reliable income	what I really like to do
a convenient time and place	

_____

_____

_____

_____

_____

_____

_____

_____

_____

_____

_____

_____

B. Reread your paragraph. Does it express your feelings and ideas clearly? Have you given examples to support what you say? Make any changes that you think are needed.

READING AND DISCUSSING

A. Discuss.

How do children communicate before they learn to speak?
What messages do they send?

B. Read the story.

The Body Language of Children

Baby's first smile! A few years ago, many people thought that a newborn baby's smile was really an expression of hurt. They thought the child had a gas pain! Now we know that a newborn baby smiles for the same reason an adult does. The child feels happy and loved! A tiny baby is curious, too. Watch an infant's eyes, and you will see that they follow you as you move around the room.

Most children take many years to speak as adults do. Until then, children have no way of telling us what they feel except through body language and through wordless sounds. Parents can learn to read this special body language and these special sounds.

Baby's first smile is a joy to see. But how about all that crying? We know the baby isn't crying just to give the parents trouble. The crying is a way of asking for help. What kind of help does the baby need? Parents have to find out.

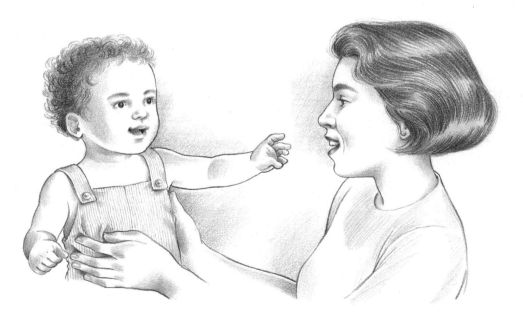

The Language of Tears

- The baby may be hungry.
- The baby may be uncomfortable. Maybe the baby's diaper needs changing. Maybe the baby feels too cold or too warm.
- The baby may be frightened by a loud noise or a new person.
- The baby may need to be touched and held. People who have studied child behavior have found out something important about the sense of touch. Babies grow anxious and nervous when no one holds them or rocks them. Loving touches are important if babies are to grow up with healthy and alert minds.
- Crying can also be a sign that the baby is sick. If the crying persists, the baby may need to see a doctor.

Many babies suffer for a time from an illness called colic. Colic is severe pain in the stomach and happens because the baby is having trouble digesting food. When babies tense their bodies and bend their legs, they are probably in pain from colic. The pain and crying go on and on, even when the baby is given warmth, food, and rocking.

Most babies outgrow colic within a few months. But in the meantime, the parents can grow tired and upset. To help them get through the baby's colicky period, wise parents sometimes ask relatives or other loving adults to help them with child care. This lets the parents rest for a few hours. When the parents come back to the baby, they are in a better mood. They can respond to the baby's pain with more love and understanding.

The Language of Success

As babies grow up, their body language is easier for adults to understand. For example, we all smile and even laugh when we are successful at a new task. Babies do this when they are able to hold up their head or roll over for the first time. Most babies are happy when they take that first walking step on their very own. Babies' body language is like that of adults. Babies' eyes get wide with joy. Their face lights up with a special smile. And—just like adults—babies feel good when they get praise and hugs from people around them.

C. Think about it.

We all have feelings of joy, pain, curiosity, and anger. How does a very young child show these feelings through body language?

behavior	communication	conscious	facial
gesture	insight	nonverbal	observe
posture	reveal		

A. Choose the correct word to complete each sentence.

1. (observe, gesture) Most parents _____ their children's body language.

2. (behavior, insight) A child's _____ can show what the child is feeling.

3. (conscious, communication) A child uses his or her body and face as a means of _____.

4. (nonverbal, posture) A smile is a _____ way of showing happiness.

5. (facial, reveal) A child's cries _____ that the child needs something.

B. Complete each sentence.

1. A baby is not always <u>conscious</u> of

   _____

2. Sometimes a child's <u>facial</u> expression is

   _____

3. A child uses hand and body <u>gestures</u>

   _____

4. Parents have <u>insight</u> into

   _____

5. A child's <u>posture</u> can reveal

   _____

Vocabulary   Prefixes and Suffixes

On page 42 of *Reading for Today Book Six*, you learned the prefix *un-* (not) and the suffix *-ness* (a state or quality). Now study a new prefix and suffix.

Prefix: *dis-* (not)
> Babies dislike wet diapers.

Suffix: *-able* (inclined or given to a state or action)
> The hot weather is unbearable.

A. Read the paragraph. Write the words with prefixes and suffixes below. (Don't write words that end with *-s* or *-es*.)

     Babies can be very sociable even though they can't talk. They communicate their wants and needs nonverbally. Their good moods are very noticeable—they smile and their eyes are open and bright. They are never dishonest about their bad moods. If they are uncomfortable, they let us know. If they don't like their food, they frown with distaste. Their parents usually can guess how they feel.

1. _____   2. _____

3. _____   4. _____

5. _____   6. _____

B. Some words have both a prefix and a suffix. (For example: *read + able = readable; un + readable = unreadable*.) Add *-able* and *un-* to each word below to make 2 new words. Then write a sentence for each.

1. (work) _____

    a. _____

    b. _____

2. (wear) _____

    a. _____

    b. _____

Reading Practice

A. Read the phrases in the box aloud. Practice until you can read them smoothly.

> 1. observe the nonverbal behavior
> 2. She had many insights
> 3. she became conscious of his posture
> 4. Donny did not stand up straight
> 5. This revealed to his mother
> 6. a child's gestures and facial expressions
> 7. They can communicate
> 8. pay more attention to Donny
> 9. This made Donny feel better

B. Write the phrases to complete the paragraph.

Fay knew how to ————————————————

1

of her son. ———————————— into his feelings.

2

When she looked at Donny, ————————————.

3

———————————— and he looked at the floor

4

as he walked. ———————————— that Donny

5

might be jealous of the baby. She knew that ————————

6

———————————— can communicate

a great deal. ———————————— fear, jealousy,

7

or love. Fay began to ————————————.

8

————————————, and he began to like the

9

new baby.

C. Read the paragraph aloud. Practice until you can read it smoothly.

Look at page 52 in *Reading for Today Book Six*. Review the meaning of subject and predicate, and the rule for forming a complete sentence. Then do the exercises below.

A. Read each sentence. Draw a line under all the words in the subject.

1. Mara was learning to walk.

2. The little girl tripped on a stone.

3. She began to cry loudly.

4. Her mother ran to comfort her.

5. A child needs a lot of comfort.

6. Now she is ready to try again.

B. Read each sentence. Draw a line under all the words in the predicate.

1. Ben was a curious five-year-old.

2. Everything interested him.

3. He liked to explore new places.

4. He asked many questions about things he saw.

5. His parents always answered his questions.

6. Little children want to know about the world.

C. Read each subject. Write a predicate to make a sentence.

1. The father _____

2. His child _____

3. Loud noises _____

4. The father and child _____

5. Fear _____

6. The child's toy _____

A. Read the story to find out more about how young children show their feelings.

The Body Language of Children

Small children have the same questions adults do. Who can I trust? Is it safe here? How can I do this hard task?

However, little children don't know how to ask these questions in words. They can only communicate their feelings through nonverbal sounds and body language. They have to depend on adults to read their sounds and body language correctly.

The Language of Jealousy

An older child usually feels jealous of a new baby. We all know the feeling of jealousy. Inside we wonder "Am I still loved? Is a new person taking my place?" A small child cannot ask these questions in words.

Little Donny often reached out his arms to his mother, Fay. Today Donny grabbed his baby brother's bottle and drank from it. This was Donny's way of saying, "If babies are so wonderful, maybe that's because they have baby bottles. I'll try that, too! Then maybe my parents will hug me more, like they used to do!"

Fay did the right thing. She observed Donny's behavior and read his body language. He needed to know that she still loved him. So she hugged him and smiled at him often. Through these gestures and facial expressions, Fay communicated to Donny that he was a very important person. Because of Fay's insight and behavior, Donny felt better. The new baby was no longer a threat to him, and he began to love his baby brother.

The Language of Touch

Fear is another feeling that we all share, no matter how young or old we are. Rita is an example. She is just one year old. She is learning how to walk, and this is hard work for her. One day as she was going along in her walker, she saw some people that she had never seen before. If Rita had been an adult, she would have asked, "Who are these new people? Why are they watching me?" Since Rita couldn't ask these questions, she expressed her uneasiness by crying.

Rita is lucky. Her parents understood that she was scared. They picked her up and hugged her. This nonverbal language let Rita know that she was safe.

Her father made gentle sounds in her ear. This let Rita know that her parents cared for her and would protect her. The next time Rita sees strangers, she probably won't cry so much.

The nonverbal language of touch is important. Children who are hugged and cuddled learn how to be caring adults. When they grow up, they know how to reach out and help other people.

Parents' Body Language

Babies and young children can also read body language. For example, Anita wanted her five-year-old son, Eric, to take his toys to his room. She stood with her hands on her hips and said in a scolding voice, "Will you pick up those toys, please?"

"I will, Mommy," Eric said, "but say it nicely." Anita repeated her request in a gentler voice, but Eric was still not pleased.

"You have to say it nicely, Mommy. That means take your hands off your hips." Eric was reading his mother's body language. Even when Anita changed her manner of speaking, her body language communicated her lack of patience.

Even toddlers of one or two years can read body language and facial expressions. They know if their parents are pleased or angry with them even if no words are spoken.

Newborn babies cannot read facial expressions and body language, but they can understand their parents' voices. A baby who hears his or her parents arguing may get very tense or start to cry. The baby knows that bad feelings are in the air.

Communication, even with babies and children, is a two-way street. They can make their needs known to us, and they can also understand what is expected of them—all nonverbally.

B. Answer the questions using complete sentences.

1. Why do very young children depend on body language for communication?

   _____

   _____

2. Why was Donny jealous of the new baby?

   _____

   _____

Comprehension

Inference

On page 50 of *Reading for Today Book Six*, you learned the steps for making inferences about a reading selection. Review those steps before practicing the skill here.

A. Reread the fourth paragraph on page 29. List the facts.

1. _____

    _____

2. _____

    _____

Which is the best inference to make about that paragraph?

○ **a.** Donny wants to drink from a bottle.
○ **b.** Donny is acting too young for his age.
○ **c.** Donny is jealous of the baby.

B. Now read this paragraph. List the facts.

  Kim was baby-sitting for little Emily for the first time. Emily looked at Kim and started to cry. She waved her fists in the air. She closed her mouth when Kim tried to give her a bottle. When Kim picked Emily up, she cried even louder.

1. _____
2. _____
3. _____
4. _____
5. _____

Which is the best inference to make?

○ **a.** Emily's diaper is wet.
○ **b.** Emily feels unhappy with a new person.
○ **c.** Emily is hungry.

From Reading to Writing

A. Many TV ads talk to children about toys and food. The people who write the ads hope the children will ask their parents to buy these things. But parents may not like the foods and toys, or may not be able to afford them. On the lines below, answer each question. You may want to use the words and phrases in the box below.

Words	Phrases
announcer	nonverbal messages
communicate	facial expressions
gestures	an unconscious effect

1. Think about an ad you've seen on TV. What is the product? What good things does the ad say about the product?

   _____

   _____

   _____

2. What kinds of body language do the people in the ad use to make the product seem wonderful?

   _____

   _____

   _____

3. Do you think this product is good for your family? Why or why not?

   _____

   _____

   _____

B. Go over the writing you did for Part A. Does each sentence have a subject and predicate? Be ready to read your answers aloud and to name a subject and predicate in each sentence.

Unit Four

Reaching Your Potential

READING AND DISCUSSING

A. Discuss.

Do you ever listen to classical music? Are you familiar with Beethoven's music?

B. Read the story.

Let the Music Play

Ludwig van Beethoven is one of the world's most famous composers of classical music. Unlike many artists, he was appreciated in his own day for his amazing achievements. Beethoven wrote many kinds of music, including instrumental, which is music written for certain musical instruments. When he began composing, that kind of music was not always well-respected. Beethoven changed all that. Thanks to him, the world now appreciates instrumental music.

Early Childhood

Ludwig was born in the city of Bonn, Germany, in 1770. That was six years before our country won its freedom from England. Ludwig's grandfather had been one of the chief musicians of his day. Ludwig's father, Johann, was also a musician, but he wasn't as talented as his father.

When Ludwig was a child, he was not considered attractive. His head was too big for his body, and his wild hair always needed combing. Even Ludwig's father made fun of his looks. As a result, Ludwig became very sensitive to the people and the world around him. His feelings were easily hurt, and he developed a bad temper.

Even as a young boy, Ludwig was sensitive to sounds. Loud, ugly sounds bothered him. He loved the soothing sound of music. When Ludwig was three, his father realized that his son had a musical gift. "Like father, like son!" he thought. "This might be a way to bring some money into the family!" Ludwig had two brothers, Johann, Jr., and Karl. However, neither of them showed much musical talent, so all the father's hopes came to rest on Ludwig.

Ludwig's father taught him to play the piano and the violin. Sometimes Ludwig made up his own tunes rather than practice the boring musical scales his father gave him. But his father got angry when Ludwig did this. Johann didn't encourage Ludwig to be creative. He only wanted his son to be a good piano player so that Ludwig could earn a living. Johann was a harsh teacher and forced Ludwig to spend hours each day practicing. At times when Johann had had too much to drink, he woke up Ludwig in the middle of the night to perform for his friends.

Although Ludwig resented his father and the hours he had to spend practicing, his love for music increased. He began to learn to play the organ from organ teachers in Bonn. At the age of eight, Ludwig gave his first public piano performance.

Vienna

At sixteen, Beethoven visited the city of Vienna, the musical capital of Europe. There he met and played for the great composer Mozart (Moat´ zart). Mozart predicted that Beethoven would become a great musician.

Seven years later, Beethoven moved to Vienna. He hated to leave his family, but he could make more money in the new city. He could send that money home to assist his brothers. In Vienna he studied with another great composer named Haydn (Hide´ n) and began to write his own music. Before long, all Vienna knew of Beethoven and was eager to hear his music.

Beethoven began to lose his hearing when he was in his late twenties. As time passed, his hearing got worse. When he finally went to a physician, he was told he would someday soon be completely deaf.

C. Think about it.

Do you think Beethoven's life became easier in time or harder? Would you like to have a talent so large that it sets you apart from others?

Vocabulary   Review

conceal	assist	dedication	resent	severe
sensitive	disability	unbearable	overcome	physician

A. Choose the correct word to complete each sentence.

1. (severe, resent) Ludwig's father was a _____ and demanding music teacher.

2. (assisted, resented) Ludwig sometimes _____ the amount of time he had to spend on practicing the piano.

3. (conceal, overcome) He tried to _____ this feeling from his father.

4. (physician, dedication) Gradually, as he practiced more and more,

   Ludwig's _____ to music grew.

5. (unbearable, disability) He began to find loud, ugly sounds

   _____.

B. Read the clues. Choose words from the word box to complete the crossword puzzle.

Down
1. lack of ability
3. rise above; get control over
6. very serious; stern

Across
2. doctor
4. easily hurt
5. help; give support

Vocabulary   Antonyms

Write a sentence for each vocabulary word and another sentence for its antonym.

1. (assist; frustrate or prevent)

   a. _____

   _____

   b. _____

   _____

2. (severe; mild)

   a. _____

   _____

   b. _____

   _____

3. (conceal; reveal)

   a. _____

   _____

   b. _____

   _____

4. (sensitive; insensitive or unfeeling)

   a. _____

   _____

   b. _____

   _____

5. (disability; ability or talent)

   a. _____

   _____

   b. _____

   _____

Reading Practice

A. Read the phrases in the box aloud. Practice until you can read them smoothly.

> 1. he started to lose his hearing
> 2. resenting his disability
> 3. He knew that no one could assist him
> 4. go on living as before
> 5. his dedication to his music increased
> 6. even though he was deaf
> 7. the vibrations of the music
> 8. he could still hear the music

B. Write the phrases to complete the paragraph.

When Beethoven was already a famous composer, _____
1

_____.

Beethoven did not waste any time _____.
2

_____
3

in writing his music. Yet he was sure that he would be able to

_____.
4

As Beethoven worked, _____
5

_____. He composed great symphonies _____
6

_____. Perhaps he could feel

_____
7

with his body. In a different way, _____
8

_____.

C. Read the paragraph aloud. Practice until you can read it smoothly.

Complete Sentences

A. Each group of words below is missing a part that would make it a complete sentence. Write the word *subject* or *predicate* to tell which part is missing.

1. Beethoven's father. _____

2. Began to lose his hearing. _____

3. Would not pay for a closed carriage. _____

4. Predicted that Beethoven would be a great success. _____

5. After riding in the open carriage, Beethoven. _____

6. Beethoven's brothers. _____

B. Change each of the phrases in A into a complete sentence on the lines below. Begin each sentence with a capital letter and end with a period.

1. _____

_____

2. _____

_____

3. _____

_____

4. _____

_____

5. _____

_____

6. _____

_____

A. Read the story to find out more about Ludwig van Beethoven's life.

Let the Music Play

The thought of life without music was unbearable to Beethoven. He decided that his disability would not change his life. He tried to conceal his deafness from the public and live his life as he always had, but that was not possible.

Beethoven continued to appear in public, but he spent most of his time writing. In the summers he went to the country outside of Vienna. He got many of his musical ideas during the long walks he'd take there. His condition grew more severe. In time, he could barely hear what someone standing right in front of him was saying.

Still, his dedication to music continued. He kept writing. It didn't matter that he could not hear the music with his ears. He heard the music inside his head and with his heart. During the next six years, he composed some of the most beautiful music the world had ever known, including his famous Fifth Symphony.

Problems Mount

As he got older, Beethoven grew more and more careless about his appearance. With his shaggy hair, tattered clothes, and moth-eaten top hat, he began to look like an old bum. During the long evening walks he liked to take, he'd talk or hum to himself, making gestures with his arms.

In time, Ludwig's parents died. So did his brother Karl. Before Karl died, he named Ludwig as the guardian of his son, also named Karl.

The boy's mother was furious. "How can you take care of my son?" she screamed at Ludwig. "You can barely take care of yourself!"

Ludwig ignored her. He made sure that his nephew Karl had everything the boy needed. He even paid to send Karl to a private school. Unfortunately, Karl was not grateful to his uncle. Karl accepted Ludwig's money and favors, but they often fought. Sometimes Ludwig was overcome with worry about Karl, and this made writing music hard for him. However, when Ludwig wrote his will, he left everything he owned to Karl.

During this time, Beethoven thought about getting married. Several times he thought he had found a wife. But in the end, Beethoven remained alone.

The Last Years

When Beethoven wrote his Ninth—and last—Symphony, he was totally deaf. It was a very long symphony and one of the greatest ever written. Beethoven had added a chorus of singers—something no composer had done before.

Beethoven himself conducted the first performance. When it was over, the audience stood and cheered wildly in the packed concert hall. Beethoven, of course, did not hear the applause—any more than he had heard the music itself.

One weekend Ludwig took Karl to visit his Uncle Johann at Johann's country home. When it was time to return to Vienna, the wind was blowing in icy blasts. Johann could have afforded to rent a warm, closed carriage for Ludwig and his nephew, but an open carriage was cheaper. Johann called for the open carriage. Ludwig did not protest. On the long ride back, freezing rain blew into the carriage. Ludwig got a chill and then a fever. Back in Vienna, his doctor told him that he had pneumonia.

Ludwig was fifty-seven. In those days, fifty-seven was considered quite old. He grew weaker and did not recover. He died of a liver disorder. As Ludwig lay dying, he raised himself a little in the bed. Perhaps he heard something—music?—in the distance. A look of joy appeared on his face. He clenched his right fist, as though in determination. Then he sank back and died.

Thirty-two years earlier, as a young man, Beethoven had written in his diary, "Courage! Despite all the weaknesses of my body, my spirit shall rule!" It was the ideal he had lived by.

B. Answer the questions using complete sentences.

1. Who predicted that Beethoven would be a successful musician?

   _____

2. What happened to Beethoven's nephew Karl when his father died?

   _____

   _____

Comprehension   Sequence

A. Write *1*, *2*, *3*, and *4* to show the order in which things happened in Beethoven's life.

_____ Beethoven moved to Vienna.

_____ He became the guardian of his nephew Karl.

_____ He began to lose his hearing.

_____ He learned to play the piano.

B. Fill in the circle beside the words that best complete each sentence.

1. Beethoven met Mozart

   ○ **a.** during his first visit to Vienna.
   ○ **b.** when he was living in Bonn.
   ○ **c.** before he learned to play the piano.

2. Beethoven learned of his disability

   ○ **a.** in his childhood.
   ○ **b.** after he moved to the countryside.
   ○ **c.** after he moved to Vienna.

C. Reread the first three paragraphs on page 39. Write a paragraph summarizing these events. Be sure to put the events in their proper order, using sequence words such as *when*, *during*, *before*, and *after*.

_____

_____

_____

_____

_____

_____

_____

_____

From Reading to Writing

A. Write a paragraph about your favorite kind of music. Tell why you enjoy it. You may want to use some of the words or phrases below.

Music Words	Phrases
country music	sensitive musician
rock music	dedication to a career
classical music	melodic, slow music
rhythm and blues	fast, loud dance music
jazz	instrumental music

_____

_____

_____

_____

_____

_____

_____

_____

_____

_____

_____

_____

_____

B. Read your paragraph. Does it express your feelings clearly? Check your sentences. Do they all have a subject and a predicate? Make any changes you think are needed.

READING AND DISCUSSING

A. Discuss.

How would you use a bank credit card?

B. Read the story.

Using Plastic

Credit cards that are issued by banks, such as *Visa* and *Mastercard*, are often called the "everything cards." With cards like these, you can walk into stores and buy clothes and furniture on credit. You can go out to eat and say, "Put it on my card." You can get money from a cash machine evenings and weekends.

The First Card

BUT . . . and it's a big BUT . . . getting your first bank card is not all that easy. The bank will ask you to fill out a credit application similar to the ones that stores give you. The bank will contact your employer to check on your income and your length of employment.

Most banks won't give you a credit card unless you've had a steady job and lived at the same address for at least a year. This proves to the bank that you are a stable person.

However, being a stable person with a good income is not usually enough to get you that first bank card. You will not get a bank card unless you already have a good credit history. This means you need to get other kinds of credit cards before you apply for a bank card. Using store charge cards and paying off a car loan are good ways of establishing a good credit history. Once you have some history of paying off debts, a bank will be more likely to consider you a good risk for a bank card.

If you don't qualify for a bank card, you may still be able to get one if you have a co-signer. A co-signer is a person who does meet all the requirements for obtaining a bank card. This person promises to pay your debt if you can't.

When the bank issues your card, the bank assigns a *credit line* to your account. A credit line is the *total debt* they think you can handle. Remember that as you're paying your monthly installments, you're also using your card to charge more things. Keep track of the amount you still owe the bank and the amount of your new charges. Don't let the total of these go above your credit line. If that should happen, you'll probably hear from your bank. Or a store clerk may check your record and refuse to let you charge anything more on that card.

Shop Around

Banks are in the credit card business to make money. If you pay your bill in installments, the bank adds interest, or a finance charge, which is the bank's monthly fee. This amount varies from bank to bank and might be 13–20 percent of the total balance you owe. If you do not pay the total balance each month, the bank charges you interest on the remaining amount. These charges can cost you a lot of money.

Every bank has a different interest policy. Some banks offer a grace period whether you pay the whole bill at once or pay in installments. The grace period is the time between the day you make a purchase and the day you have to start paying interest. However, many banks start charging interest from the day you make your purchase, even if you pay the balance when the bill comes.

Before you choose a credit card, ask these questions:

- <u>What is the annual interest rate?</u> The bank that issues the card sets the interest rate, not the card company. So if you want a *Visa* card, for example, you should check several banks and choose the one offering the lowest interest rate for *Visa* cards.
- <u>What is the yearly fee?</u> (This is a once-a-year flat fee.) Again, this fee varies from bank to bank.
- <u>Is there a grace period before interest charges start?</u>

If you get a bank credit card and use it wisely, your credit rating will go up. You'll find it easier to get other bank cards. Those plastic cards can open doors for you. Just remember that when you say "Charge it," *you're* supposed to be in charge!

C. Think about it.

What are some of the pros and cons of having a bank credit card? Why is it a good idea to keep a record of your bank credit card charges each month?

Vocabulary Review

apply	accurate	establish	financial	installment
notify	obligation	previous	qualify	reference

A. Choose the correct word to complete each sentence.

1. (reference, apply) If you want a charge card, you will have to

    _____ for one.

2. (notify, financial) You will have to fill out a _____
    statement.

3. (accurate, references) The store will probably check your

    _____ .

4. (previous, qualify) They might call your _____
    creditors.

5. (installments, establish) When you get the charge card, you will

    be able to pay for products in _____ .

B. Use the new vocabulary words in your own sentences.

1. Establishing a good credit record _____

    _____ .

2. _____

    _____ your obligations.

3. _____

    _____ qualify for a credit card.

4. _____

    _____ accurate records.

5. The bank will notify _____

    _____ .

Vocabulary — Prefixes and Suffixes

On page 78 of *Reading for Today Book Six*, you learned the suffixes *–er* and *–or* (one who). Now study a new prefix and suffix.

Prefix: *en–* (to cause to be)
Sometimes it is necessary to enlist the services of a debt counselor.

Suffix: *–ment* (result of an action; a condition)
Getting the first credit card is quite an accomplishment.

A. Read the paragraph. Write the words with prefixes and suffixes below.

Janice just received her first bank card. To her amazement, she was given a credit line of $1,000. She felt good because this extra money would help her to make some improvements in her life. She would be able to enlarge her wardrobe and go on a trip. She knew she would also have to enforce some self-control when she went shopping. She didn't want to become a big spender or start buying more than she could afford. Building a good credit record would be an achievement that would help her later.

1. _____   2. _____

3. _____   4. _____

5. _____   6. _____

B. Write sentences for three of the words you listed in exercise A.

1. _____

_____

2. _____

_____

3. _____

_____

A. **Read the phrases in the box aloud. Practice until you can read them smoothly.**

> 1. didn't have any previous debts
> 2. They had no references
> 3. The Jarvises would have to establish
> 4. to apply for a charge card
> 5. an accurate financial statement
> 6. they qualified for a charge card

B. **Write the phrases to complete the paragraph.**

Since Linda and Ed _____
_____ 1

_____, they couldn't get a loan to buy a

house. _____ that
_____ 2

the loan officer at the bank could check. _____
_____ 3

_____

a good credit history before they could get such a big loan. They

went to a department store _____
_____ 4

_____. They supplied the credit manager with

_____.
_____ 5

The credit manager decided that _____
_____ 6

_____. Linda and Ed used

the card to get some things they needed for their apartment. Every

month they paid the bill from the store and began building a good

credit rating.

C. **Read the paragraph aloud. Practice until you can read it smoothly.**

Writing Skills — Past Tense of Verbs

Review what you learned about the past tenses of verbs on page 88 in *Reading for Today Book Six*. Then complete the exercises.

A. Complete the chart.

Present	Past	Past Participle
fight		has fought
seek	sought	
	kept	has kept
stand		has stood
bring	brought	

B. Write the correct past verb form in each sentence.

1. (give) The bank had _____ the customer a new credit card.

2. (write) She _____ her name on it when she got the card.

3. (see) At that time she _____ that the card had a date on it.

4. (forget) She had _____ that new cards are sent every year or two.

5. (throw) When the new card came, she _____ away the old card.

6. (keep) The customer _____ her new card in her wallet.

7. (bring) She has _____ the card with her today.

8. (see) She had _____ the ad for a sale in the paper.

A. Read the story to find out more about bank credit cards.

Using Plastic

Once you receive your first bank card and start charging purchases on it, you begin to build up a credit history. If you establish a reputation for paying your debts and having a good credit history, you may be able to get many other credit cards. The first card may be hard to get, but having one card makes getting additional cards easier. The payments you make on that first card become part of your credit history. Many people with a good credit record receive applications for additional cards in the mail.

In Too Deep

Something like that happened to Sheila and Mark Kaplan. They had been married a few years, and they each had a good job. Mark was a nurse, and Sheila worked as a computer operator. Since they each had been working at the same job for almost two years, they had no trouble getting that first bank card. The Kaplans knew they would be paying around 18 percent interest, but the convenience was worth it. The bank card also enabled them to buy some large items that they couldn't have gotten without saving for six months to a year.

Then the Kaplans started getting applications for other bank cards. Now that they had established a good credit record, other banks were eager to get their business. Soon the Kaplans had ten credit cards. That was very exciting. Suddenly, they could have anything they wanted. They began to buy things that they didn't really need, such as $500 worth of clothes. They went to more expensive restaurants and planned to go to Mexico on vacation.

The Kaplans continued to pay the minimum amount due on their credit card bills every month, but they didn't realize that they were spending much more than they were paying back. When they reached their credit limit on one card, they just used another card. When they began to use one credit card to pay money due on another card, they realized that they were in debt over their heads.

By then, Sheila and Mark were thousands of dollars in debt. They had to get rid of all their credit cards. Then they lived on a very strict budget for several years in order to pay off all their debts. They decided that their brief fling of buying anything they wanted was not worth the result.

Safe But Sorry

Ed and Linda Jarvis lived at the opposite extreme. They, too, had good jobs where they had worked for several years. However, they believed in living within their means. Neither Linda nor Ed had any bank cards or store charge cards. If they bought something, they always paid for it in cash. If they couldn't afford something, they saved for it. They didn't feel they were missing out on anything. When they wanted something badly enough, they could always figure out a way to get it.

After the Jarvises had been married for several years, they decided to buy a house. This is when their problems began. Since they'd always bought with cash, they didn't have a credit history. The bank where they applied for a loan couldn't find out if they were a good risk.

"But we've never been in debt," Ed pointed out. "Shouldn't that prove that we're a good credit risk?" No, that was not enough for the loan officer. She couldn't predict whether the Jarvises would pay monthly installments promptly. They would have to get a charge card and pay the debt on time before a bank would loan them a larger amount of money.

Living with credit may be just as difficult as living without it. Television and magazine ads often encourage us to spend beyond our means. If we do that, we may end up like Sheila and Mark. Yet if we spend only the cash we have and are never in debt like Linda and Ed, we may not get a credit line when we really need it. Those people who can use credit wisely have the best of both worlds.

B. Answer each question using a complete sentence.

1. Why is getting a second or third credit card easier than getting the first? _____

_____

2. How did Mark and Sheila Kaplan get over their heads in debt?

_____

_____

Comprehension   **Conclusions**

On page 86 of *Reading for Today Book Six*, you learned the steps for drawing conclusions about a reading selection. Review those steps before practicing the skill here.

A. Read the first paragraph under "Shop Around" on page 44. Then list the facts.

1. _____

2. _____

3. _____

Which is the best conclusion to draw from the facts?

    ○ **a.** Interest charges vary from bank to bank.

    ○ **b.** You may pay interest as high as 20 percent.

    ○ **c.** Using a bank card costs money.

B. Now read this paragraph. List four important facts.

    Darleen ran into the house and went straight to her desk. She opened the top drawer where she kept her most important papers. After she pushed some papers around, she found what she was looking for: the list of her credit cards and the account number of each one. She breathed a sigh of relief and reached for the telephone.

1. _____

2. _____

3. _____

4. _____

Which is the best conclusion to draw from the facts?

    ○ **a.** Darleen lost her credit cards and wants to report the loss immediately.

    ○ **b.** There's a big sale, and Darleen wants to go shopping.

    ○ **c.** Darleen wants to lend her credit cards to her best friend.

A. Did you ever try to buy something on credit? What problems, if any, did you have? What did you learn? Write about an experience you had while buying on credit. You might want to use some of the words and phrases in the box below.

Words	Phrases
creditor	taking on debts and obligations
establish	to qualify for credit
interest	an accurate record of my finances
installment	my advice to shoppers

_____

_____

_____

_____

_____

_____

_____

_____

_____

_____

_____

_____

_____

B. Review your paragraph. Did you tell about things in the order in which they happened? Did you use the correct past tense forms of verbs? Make any changes that you think will improve your story.

READING AND DISCUSSING

A. Discuss.

What teams are you a member of? What makes a team function well?

B. Read the story.

Teamwork on the Job

Working as a Team

Li Chen rushed into the apartment and threw her coat on the sofa. "I have important news!" she told her husband. "I've been selected as a team leader at the plant!"

"What team? Slow down and tell me from the beginning."

"The managers have decided to organize the workers in teams of five. Instead of each of us having to meet his or her own quota, the team as a unit has to meet its quota. If the team produces well, the whole team will receive a bonus. Because I'm a ten-year employee, I'll be a team leader."

"Terrific! Do you know yet who will be on your team?"

"Hector, Loretta, Calvin, and the new woman, Mercedes. Loretta and Calvin have both worked on the line for a long time, so I'm not concerned about them—they understand the job. Hector has been there for about a year, and Mercedes started last week. I just hope Loretta and Calvin won't be resentful because I was selected as team leader."

"Will you be their supervisor?"

"Oh, no. I'll just be the one who coordinates the team. Everyone on the team will be equal."

An Unexpected Problem

The next day Li Chen was glad to go to the plant. During the morning, she thought about the other members of her team. Were they also excited? Were they working quickly enough? She glanced at Hector. He was working with a steady rhythm. Li Chen dreamed happily about the bonus they would all share.

Soon it was time for the morning break. Calvin approached her at the water cooler. "I'm afraid we have a problem," he said.

"Is Mercedes working too slowly?"

"No, our problem is Loretta."

"But Loretta has been working on the line for years!"

"I know, but now she's working very slowly, and she's making careless mistakes. It's your responsibility to straighten her out."

"Let's wait until the end of the week when we get the production figures from management. In the meantime, you and Hector and I can work a little faster to compensate for her."

"That's not fair!" said Calvin. "Why should I have to work harder to do someone else's job? In the old days if I worked harder, I got a bonus. Now I have to work harder for nothing because Loretta is not doing her share."

"I guess we need to have a team meeting on Friday," Li Chen sighed. "Will you come?"

"I'll come," said Calvin, "but I don't know what good it'll do."

An Angry Meeting

On Friday the team met. Li Chen took a deep breath and said, "I have terrible news: we didn't make our quota for this week." Mercedes looked down and blushed. She thought this was her fault.

"No, Mercedes, it isn't you," said Li Chen. "The foreman has been monitoring you because you're new, and he told me you're doing fine."

"We all know that it's Loretta who's dragging the team down," said Calvin.

"Me!" said Loretta. "I'm the one who's carrying you people!"

"Calvin is right, Loretta," said Hector. "You punch in late every morning; then you come back late from lunch. Even when you're working, it seems like you're hardly paying attention."

"I'm paying more attention than you are!" said Loretta. "I do my own work, instead of spying on other people!"

"That's enough," said Li Chen. "Let's concentrate on how to make our quota next week. Let's figure out what we need to do."

"I'm doing everything I can," said Loretta, "so I don't need to talk about it!" She picked up her coat and stormed out of the room.

The rest of the team looked at each other. "Great job, team leader," Calvin said.

After the meeting, Li Chen walked home slowly. *I wish I had never been chosen as team leader!* she thought. *What can I do?*

C. Think About It

What would you do if you were in Li Chen's place? Would you resign as team leader? Would you report Loretta to management? Try to think of a solution that would be fair to everyone.

Vocabulary Review

conditions	emotions	environment	hostile	offensive
constitute	harassment	promotion	representative	supervisor

A. Choose the correct word to complete each sentence.

1. (environment, offensive) The right office _____ can encourage workers.

2. (supervisor, promotion) Employees expect a _____ when they do good work.

3. (representative, emotions) Workers may hide their _____ when a boss doesn't want to hear about them.

4. (constitute, harassment) Responsibility and sharing are what _____ good feelings among employees.

5. (hostile, conditions) When workers get _____ and withdrawn, production can suffer.

B. Complete each sentence.

1. Good office <u>conditions</u> help employees to _____
_____.

2. Many workers find it <u>offensive</u> when _____
_____.

3. In team management, each employee is a <u>representative</u> of _____
_____.

4. In a team setting, <u>harassment</u> is less _____
_____.

5. With team management, the role of <u>supervisor</u> may _____
_____.

A. Read each analogy. After it write *means the same*, *opposites*, *part to whole*, or *use or function* to identify the relationship.

1. *Worker* is to *employee* as *supervisor* is to *manager*.

   _____

2. *Telephone* is to *conversation* as *piano* is to *music*.

   _____

3. *Promotion* is to *firing* as *problem* is to *solution*.

   _____

4. *Member* is to *team* as *door* is to *building*.

   _____

B. Write the word that completes each analogy.

1. *Argument* is to *agreement* as *hostile* is to _____.

   office   unkind   friendly

2. *Assist* is to *help* as *halt* is to _____.

   go   harass   stop

3. *Movie* is to *entertainment* as *school* is to _____.

   vacation   learning   teacher

4. *Trust* is to *doubt* as *compete* is to _____.

   cooperate   strive   wonder

5. *Sad* is to *gloomy* as *joy* is to _____.

   prize   sorrow   gladness

6. *Knife* is to *butter* as *spoon* is to _____.

   soup   silver   table

7. *Letter* is to *word* as *word* is to _____.

   belief   sentence   sound

A. Read the phrases in the box aloud. Practice until you can read them smoothly.

> 1. a healthy work environment
> 2. to make major decisions
> 3. has a stake in making the decisions work
> 4. becomes a representative of the company
> 5. take turns supervising work output
> 6. make decisions about promotions and pay raises

B. Write the phrases to complete the paragraph.

Teamwork usually builds _____
_____ 1

_____. When workers pitch in _____
2

_____, each person _____
3

_____.

In fact, each worker _____
4

_____.

In many offices, workers _____
5

_____. They may also

_____
6

_____.

C. Read the paragraph aloud. Practice until you can read it smoothly.

I	me	you	he	him	she
her	it	we	us	they	them

A. Read the sentences below. Circle each pronoun. Then write the word that the circled pronoun stands for.

1. Joan decided that she was in a rut at work. _____

2. "I feel the same way," said Warren. _____

3. Decisions got made, but Joan didn't take part in them.

   _____

4. Warren said he felt left out, too. _____

5. The boss always said to Warren, "Here you just follow orders!"

   _____

6. Warren talked with Joan and helped her make a decision.

   _____

B. Write a pronoun to use in place of the underlined words below.

1. Warren and Joan went job hunting. _____

2. The search was long, but the search paid off. _____

3. Joan told Warren, "This office uses teamwork!" _____

4. Joan likes her coworkers. "Employees get along well here,"

   she said. _____

5. The team manager presented Warren's team with a problem.

   "Leave it to the team to solve!" said Warren. _____

6. "If it was up to Joan," laughed Joan, "I'd work here all my life!"

   _____

Comprehension

A. **Read the story to find out more about working as a team.**

Teamwork on the Job

On Monday Li Chen felt horrible. Loretta and Calvin turned away from her, and Hector gave her a hopeless look. At lunch Mercedes came over to her timidly. "I think I know what's wrong with Loretta," she said.

"What do you mean?" asked Li Chen.

"After the meeting on Friday, I was walking home past a bar. I saw Loretta inside, so I went in and ordered a club soda. Everyone there knew Loretta. She tried to order another drink, but the bartender told her she'd already had enough. I started to tell Loretta about my uncle back in Peru who had a drinking problem. She got very angry at me. She said she didn't have a drinking problem. That's what my uncle said, too."

"A drinking problem would explain the change in her," said Li Chen. "Loretta was an excellent worker. Maybe she got depressed and started drinking. I wonder what happened?"

"I don't know," Mercedes said, shrugging. "She wouldn't open up to me, but maybe she would confide in you."

Help for Loretta

That evening Li Chen went to the bar where Mercedes had found Loretta on Friday. Sure enough, Loretta was there again. Li Chen sat down next to her.

"Loretta, I'm sorry we were so hard on you on Friday."

"Well," said Loretta, "it's over now."

"No, it's not over," said Li Chen. "Things won't get better until you get help for your problem. I'm telling you this because I care about you. You used to be an excellent worker, but now you are not. I can't let you bring the whole team down. If you agree, we can get the company to help you, and you can become a good worker again."

"The company doesn't care about me."

"You're wrong about that. All employees are important to the company. That's why they have an employee assistance program. You can go to the hospital for a month. The doctors there will help you stop drinking. While you're gone, there will be a temporary employee on our team. When you come back in a month, your old job will be available for you and you can keep it as long as you do the work. Your insurance will cover most of the bills, so it won't cost you much."

"Well, the doctors might cure my drinking problem, but I'll never be happy again. I'm so depressed."

"What are you talking about, Loretta? What happened?"

"My boyfriend, Clayton, took off. I came home one day and all his things were gone. He left me a note that he wouldn't be back."

"Oh, Loretta, I'm sorry. If you had told me, I might have helped. I would have understood what was wrong. Please go to the personnel director tomorrow morning and tell her you want to start the employee assistance program right away. Drinking is no way to deal with your problems. Then come and talk to me. You don't have to face this alone."

A Winning Team

The next morning Li Chen explained to the team that Loretta was entering the employee assistance program and would be gone for a month. She also told them about Loretta's problem with her boyfriend.

"Loretta's had a hard time," said Calvin.

"Yes," Hector agreed. "That could happen to any of us."

A month later when Loretta returned to work, she looked rested and well.

"I want to apologize for my behavior," Calvin told her. "Instead of yelling at you, I should have been trying to find out what was wrong."

"It's forgotten," said Loretta. "I should have shared my problem with the team instead of trying to forget it by drinking."

Soon there was another team meeting. Li Chen smiled at the team and held up a check. "This is our bonus," she said. "Let's vote on how to share it! Our team is number one!"

B. Answer the questions using complete sentences.

1. How did Li Chen find out what might be affecting Loretta's work?

_____

_____

2. Why was Loretta depressed? _____

_____

3. What happened when Loretta rejoined the team? _____

_____

Comprehension   Writer's Tone and Purpose

On page 104 of *Reading for Today Book Six,* you learned the steps for recognizing a writer's tone and purpose. Review those steps before practicing the skill here.

Read this letter and fill in the circle next to the answer that bests completes each sentence.

> Dear Ms. Lin:
>
> I believe that my supervisor is treating me unfairly because I am a woman. I work the same hours as my male coworkers, and I produce as much as they do. Yet I am not paid as much as men who do the same job, and I am passed over for promotion. I would like to make an appointment with you to discuss this matter.
>
> Sincerely,
>
> *Tina Livingston*

1. The writer's purpose is to

   ○ **a.** complain about working conditions.
   ○ **b.** let management know that she is being treated unfairly.
   ○ **c.** describe the kind of work she wants to do.

2. The writer achieves this purpose by

   ○ **a.** blaming her coworkers.
   ○ **b.** blaming the company.
   ○ **c.** stating the facts and asking for an appointment.

3. The tone of the letter is

   ○ **a.** firm.
   ○ **b.** sad.
   ○ **c.** humorous.

4. What conclusion can you reach after reading Tina's letter?

   ○ **a.** She feels free to communicate with management.
   ○ **b.** She is a poor worker.
   ○ **c.** She doesn't know how to work with a team.

From Reading to Writing

A. People have different opinions and feelings about work conditions. Some people like working in a team. Other people like working alone. Write a paragraph about the work condition that suits you best. You may want to use some of the words and phrases below.

Words	Phrases
independent	the value of privacy
cooperation	encouragement and praise
commitment	making decisions

_____

_____

_____

_____

_____

_____

_____

_____

_____

_____

_____

_____

_____

B. Read your paragraph. Does it express your ideas clearly? Have you given examples to support what you say? Make any changes that you think are needed.

From Reading to Writing

A. Think back to a problem in a place where you worked. Write about it. In your writing, respond to these questions:

- What was the problem?

- What caused the problem?

- Was the problem solved? If so, how was it solved?

- If the problem wasn't solved, give your ideas for solving it.

_____

_____

_____

_____

_____

_____

_____

_____

_____

_____

_____

_____

_____

_____

_____

_____

B. Read what you've written. Have you expressed your ideas clearly? Have you given details to make your point clear? Make any changes that you think are needed.

READING AND DISCUSSING

A. **Discuss**.

Why is it important to take pride in your work? Why is respect often as meaningful as money?

B. **Read the story**.

The Gift of Giving

Some people become famous because of their achievements as singers, dancers, or actors. Others are good at sports, painting, or writing. Still others are great leaders of governments or successful business executives. Many people become well-known because they are really rich, good looking, or very social.

Oseola McCarty became known to the world for other reasons. She gave her life savings away so that needy students could go to the University of Southern Mississippi. What was so unusual about that? As it turned out, everything!

A Working Childhood

Oseola McCarty, called Ola, was born in Mississippi in 1908. She spent her childhood in Hattiesburg with her mother, aunt, and grandmother. The women did other people's washing and ironing to make their living. The work was hard, and the pay was poor. Although the women lived in poverty, they still took great pride in their work. Ola's grandmother even made her own soap.

At first Ola went to school and helped out when she got home. Even then, she showed great discipline about money. "I would go to school and come home and iron," she told an interviewer years later. "I'd put money away and save it."

When Ola was in the sixth grade, her aunt got very sick. Ola's help with the laundry was needed even more. She dropped out of school and never went back.

A Working Life

From then on Ola worked six days a week. At first customers paid only one dollar and fifty cents to two dollars for a bundle of laundry. In time the price went up to ten dollars. Ola continued to put her money in the bank, dollar by dollar.

In 1944, Ola's grandmother died. By 1967, both her mother and aunt were gone, too. Now Ola was alone. She went on washing and ironing and living as before in the family's little house in Hattiesburg. She didn't buy a lot of things. She never owned a car. To get food, she walked a mile to the store. The only other place she ever went was to church.

During these years Ola lived a very quiet life. People dropped by to leave their clothes, but rarely stayed to chat. She had a few pets and sometimes talked to them. She spent her days among the piles of laundry waiting to be washed and ironed and the rows of clothes drying on the line.

A Big Idea

As Ola got older, she began to think about what she should do with her savings. She wanted to leave some money to her cousins and some to her church. But she decided that her biggest charity would be the University of Southern Mississippi. Although the college was right in Ola's hometown, she had never been there. Still, Ola said, "They used to not let colored people go out there, but now they do, and I think they should have it [the money]." Like most colleges in the South, USM did not accept black students until the laws changed and required schools to take students of all races.

Ola's idea was to start a scholarship fund to help black students go to USM. "I just want the scholarship to go to some child who needs it," she said. "I'm too old to get an education, but they can."

And so, at the age of 87, Ola McCarty left her life savings— $150,000—for scholarships to a school she had never even seen.

C. Think about it.

What value did Ola McCarty put on work? How did she value education? How do you think people reacted to her gift?

poverty	executive	discipline	challenge
achievement	legend	charity	empathy
literacy	spirituality		

A. Choose the correct word to complete each sentence.

1. (legend, literacy) Ola McCarty wanted a deserving student to have a chance at real _____.

2. (poverty, charity) A college education is a way out of _____.

3. (executive, achievement) Ola spoke to an _____ at her bank about her plan.

4. (empathy, discipline) People were amazed at her _____ in saving money.

5. (challenge, legend) Ola's gift made her a _____ at the college.

B. Read the clues. Choose words from the word box to complete the puzzle.

Down
1. giving to the poor
3. deed accomplished
4. training of character

Across
2. entering someone's feelings
5. devotion to spiritual things
6. being poor
7. a test

Vocabulary   Prefixes

A. Read the base word. Then circle the related word in the sentence.

1. verbal   The women's communication was nonverbal.

2. justice   At that time black people suffered many injustices.

3. able   Ola was unable to finish school.

4. possible   People thought it was impossible for her to save so
   much money.

5. like   Did she dislike the life she led?

B. Complete the sentence with the word that makes it correct. Then write the words you circled in A above.

In the sentences above, the prefixes *un–*, *in–*, *im–*, *non–* and *dis–*

all mean _____ .

_____

_____

C. Read each word. Then use it in a sentence of your own.

1. unpopular _____

_____

2. incomplete _____

_____

3. impatient _____

_____

4. nonviolent _____

_____

5. disagree _____

_____

A. Read the phrases in the box aloud. Practice until you can read them smoothly.

1. the challenges
2. a sense of spirituality and discipline
3. empathy for students who came from poverty
4. which provided literacy
5. made Ola a legend
6. from all walks of life
7. by her charity

B. Write the phrases to complete the paragraph.

Ola McCarty met ———————————— of her life

with ————————————————————————

————————————. Her gift showed ————————

   1

   2

   3

————————————————————————. This gift

of her life savings, ————————————————

   4

for others, ————————————. People

   5

————————————— were inspired

   6

—————————.

   7

C. Read the paragraph aloud. Practice until you can read it smoothly.

Recognizing Run-ons

A. Rewrite these run-ons to form two new sentences.

1. By the time she was 87, Ola could no longer work her hands were bent and worn from washing other people's clothes.

   _____

   _____

2. Ola McCarty was an independent woman she lived alone for most of her adult life.

   _____

   _____

3. Ola saved her money, dollar by dollar few people knew she had such a fortune.

   _____

   _____

4. As a girl, Ola gave up her education to help support her family she took care of her relatives when they were ill.

   _____

   _____

B. Rewrite the paragraph so it has at least four complete sentences.

   People at her bank helped Ola invest her savings they also figured out a plan to look after her when she could no longer work. They even helped her get an air conditioner Ola only used it when visitors came to her house.

   _____

   _____

   _____

   _____

   _____

   _____

A. Read the story below to find out more about Oseola McCarty.

The Gift of Giving

When Ola McCarty gave her gift to the university in 1995, people were greatly surprised. How could a washerwoman do something like this? Where did she get the money? Why was she so generous?

But no one was more surprised by what happened than Ola McCarty. All of a sudden, she was the center of attention. Everyone wanted to hear her story. Reporters came from all over to talk to her. Stories about her appeared in newspapers and magazines and on TV.

Making a Difference

People at the University of Southern Mississippi were greatly moved by Ola's charity. "This is just extraordinary," said the school's president. "I don't know that I have ever been as touched by a gift as I am by this one. Miss McCarty has shown great unselfishness and sensitivity in making possible for others the education she never had."

For Stephanie Bullock, Oseola's gift made an immediate difference. Stephanie was the first student to receive an Oseola McCarty Scholarship. Stephanie also got to know the woman behind the gift and came to think of her as "another grandmother." Stephanie soon appreciated Miss Ola's spirituality and empathy. She said, "Her act was not a quest for fame. The gift was genuine good old-fashioned kindness that perfectly reflected the kind of person Miss Ola was."

A New Life

Ola McCarty's last years were very busy ones. Overnight she had become a legend. Not only was she featured in the news, but many important people wanted to meet her. She even had dinner with the President of the United States.

Miss Ola also received many awards. She was given the Presidential Citizens medal. The National Urban League made her a "Community Hero," Harvard University honored her, and best of all, her picture was hung in a building at USM.

At first, Ola was afraid to fly, so she took the train to all the places that wanted her. Then she got bolder and began taking airplanes. Before her fame, Ola had been out of Mississippi only once. Suddenly, she was traveling all over the country. "I want to see," she said. "I want to know."

Her Story in Books

As Oseola traveled, people recorded what she said. Soon a book of her sayings was published. It's called *Oseola McCarty's Simple Wisdom for Rich Living*. Each page gives Ola's thoughts on the challenges of life. For example, on self-esteem she says: "It seems pretty basic to me. If you want to feel proud of yourself, you've got to do things you can be proud of."

A children's book about Ola came out, too. It's called *The Riches of Oseola McCarty*. This book tells the life story of an American legend. It also tells how to set up a savings plan!

The Giving Goes On

Oseola McCarty died in 1999 at the age of 91. By the time of her death, she had received more than 300 awards. Her gift to help improve the literacy of students had turned into a much bigger achievement. Many people had added their contributions to her scholarship fund so that more students could get aid. Many others were inspired by her message that no matter what their background, people can always do something to help someone else.

Perhaps Stephanie Bullock put it best. "Her gift was so much more than financial assistance. It told the world that people with good intentions still exist. I hope to live a life comparable to hers."

B. **Answer each question using a complete sentence.**

1. What were some of the obstacles that Oseola McCarty had to overcome in her life?

   _____

   _____

2. Why were people so touched by Oseola McCarty's gift?

   _____

   _____

3. How did Oseola's gift come back to her?

   _____

   _____

Comprehension   Fact vs. Opinion

A. Each sentence below contains a fact and an opinion. Underline the fact and circle the opinion.

1. Oseola McCarty and her family were poor so they were probably unhappy.

2. The women in Ola's family took in laundry because it was most likely the only thing they could do.

3. Ola saved money instead of spending it, so she probably didn't care for material things.

4. Ola lived a quiet life because she didn't care about people.

5. *Oseola McCarty's Simple Wisdom for Rich Living* was published in 1996 and is the best book of its kind.

B. Reread the story about Oseola McCarty. Then answer these questions.

1. What was the president of the University of Southern Mississippi's opinion of Oseola?

   _____

   _____

2. What was Oseola McCarty's opinion about education?

   _____

   _____

3. How do you think the writer of the story feels about Oseola McCarty?

   _____

   _____

From Reading to Writing

A. You have read about a woman who never complained about the work she did, but instead took pride in doing it well. Write a paragraph about a positive attitude that you have about one of the following topics or another topic that is meaningful to you.

1. giving to or working for a charity
2. the value of literacy and education
3. finding spirituality in your life
4. exercising discipline in what you do
5. meeting the challenges that come your way
6. setting goals and achievements that are important to you

_____

_____

_____

_____

_____

_____

_____

_____

_____

_____

_____

_____

_____

B. Go over your paragraph by reading it to yourself. Does it present your opinions accurately? Have you made your ideas clear to your reader? Make any changes that you think are needed.

Answer Key

Unit One

Page 5   **A.** 1. audiences 2. passionate
3. influenced 4. commitment 5. published
B. *Across* 1. creative 3. published
4. passionate 7. commitment 8. influence
9. recognition *Down* 2. relative 5. audience
6. reminisce 7. culture

Page 6   1. d 2. a 3. c 4. e 5. b 6. d 7. c
8. b 9. a

Page 8   **A.** 1. creative 2. passionate
3. famous 4. important 5. powerful 6. lively
B. 1. interesting 2. believable 3. careful
4. exciting 5. big **C.** Answers will vary.

Page 10   **B.** 1. They are called characters
and settings. 2. They take place in his old
neighborhood in Pittsburgh. 3. *Ma Rainey's
Black Bottom, Fences, Joe Turner's Come and
Gone,* or *The Piano Lesson* 4. Wilson sees
conflict in connecting with traditions of the
past, surviving in the present, and moving
into the future.

Page 11   **A.** 1. b, c 2. a, b **B.** Answers
will vary.

Unit Two

Page 15   **A.** 1. ambition 2. reliable 3. access
4. productive **B.** *Across* 3. productive 6. live
8. star 9. circulars 10. stay *Down* 1. frequently
2. edge 4. inventory 5. accuracy 7. access
8. sick

Page 16   **A.** 1. d 2. j 3. b 4. h 5. a 6. g 7. i
8. e 9. c 10. f **B.** 1. de(sert); f 2. con(tent); i
3. ob(ject); c 4. pro(duce); e 5. (de)sert; b
6. (con)tents; d 7. re(fuse); g 8. (pro)duce; j

Page 18   **A.** Angela's Cafe; Los Angeles,
California; The Garden Show; Ms. Linda
Torez; New Year's Day; Kent City Journal
B. 1. Carmen moved from Pen Street to a
larger apartment on Worth Avenue.
2. The new apartment was near Fairfield
Community College and Jiffy Food Mart.
3. On Saturdays and Sundays, Carmen
walked to the park with Floyd and Maria.

Page 20   **B.** 1. Elsa offered Carmen a job
behind the desk at a motel. 2. They seemed
surprised, because they all said "A nursery!"
at once. 3. (Answers will vary.) Example:
She has always liked the feeling she has at a
nursery, and she likes working with plants.

Page 21   **A.** 1. a 2. c 3. b **B.** 1. c 2. a 3. b

Unit Three

Page 25   **A.** 1. observe 2. behavior
3. communication 4. nonverbal 5. reveal
B. Answers will vary.

Page 26   **A.** 1. sociable 2. nonverbally
3. noticeable 4. dishonest 5. uncomfortable
6. distaste **B.** 1. workable, unworkable
2. wearable, unwearable

Page 28   **A.** 1. Mara 2. The little girl
3. She 4. Her mother 5. A child 6. she
B. 1. was a curious five-year-old 2. interested
him 3. liked to explore new places 4. asked
many questions about things he saw 5. always
answered his questions 6. want to know
about the world **C.** Answers will vary but
should all contain a verb.

Page 30   **B.** 1. They don't know how to
talk yet. 2. He thought the baby had all his
mother's love.

Page 31   **A.** 1. Donny reached out to his
mother. 2. He grabbed the baby's bottle and
drank from it.; c **B.** 1. Kim was babysitting
for Emily for the first time. 2. Emily looked
at Kim and started to cry. 3. She waved her
fists. 4. Emily wouldn't eat when Kim tried
to feed her. 5. When Kim picked Emily up,
she cried even louder.; b

Unit Four

Page 35   **A.** 1. severe 2. resented
3. conceal 4. dedication 5. unbearable
B. *Down* 1. disability 3. overcome 6. severe
Across 2. physician 4. sensitive 5. assist

Page 36   Answers will vary.

Page 38   **A.** 1. predicate 2. subject
3. subject 4. subject 5. predicate 6. predicate
B. Answers will vary.

Page 40 **B.** 1. Mozart predicted that Beethoven would be a successful musician. 2. Beethoven became his nephew's guardian.

Page 41 **A.** 2; 4; 3; 1 **B.** 1. a 2. c **C.** Answers will vary.

Unit Five

Page 45 **A.** 1. apply 2. financial 3. references 4. previous 5. installments **B.** Answers will vary.

Page 46 **A.** 1. amazement 2. improvements 3. enlarge 4. enforce 5. spender 6. achievement **B.** Answers will vary.

Page 48 **A.** fought; has sought; keep; stood; has brought **B.** 1. given 2. wrote 3. saw 4. forgotten 5. threw 6. kept 7. brought 8. seen

Page 50 **B.** 1. You can use your first card as part of your credit record. 2. The Kaplans did not keep track of how much they were spending, and they bought things they didn't need.

Page 51 **A.** 1. Banks are in the credit card business to make money. 2. Banks add a finance charge to your bill. 3. The amount of interest varies from bank to bank.; c **B.** 1. Darleen went straight to her desk. 2. She looked for something in the top drawer. 3. She found a list of credit card accounts. 4. She reached for the telephone.; a

Unit Six

Page 55 **A.** 1. environment 2. promotion 3. emotions 4. constitute 5. hostile **B.** Answers will vary.

Page 56 **A.** 1. means the same 2. use or function 3. opposites 4. part to whole **B.** 1. friendly 2. stop 3. learning 4. cooperate 5. gladness 6. soup 7. sentence

Page 58 **A.** 1. she, Joan 2. I, Warren 3. them, Decisions 4. he, Warren 5. you, Warren 6. her, Joan **B.** 1. They 2. it 3. him 4. We 5. us 6. me

Page 60 **B.** 1. Mercedes told Li Chen she saw Loretta at a bar. Later Li Chen went to the bar and talked to Loretta. 2. Her boyfriend Clayton took off. 3. They received a bonus.

Page 61 1. b 2. c 3. a 4. a

Unit Seven

Page 66 **A.** 1. literacy 2. poverty 3. executive 4. discipline 5. legend **B.** *Down* 1. charity 3. achievement 4. discipline *Across* 2. empathy 5. spirituality 6. poverty 7. challenge

Page 67 **A.** 1. nonverbal 2. injustices 3. unable 4. impossible 5. dislike **B.** not **C.** Answers will vary.

Page 69 **A.** 1. By the time she was 87, Ola could no longer work. Her hands were bent and worn from washing other people's clothes. 2. Ola McCarty was an independent woman. She lived alone for most of her adult life. 3. Ola saved her money, dollar by dollar. Few people knew she had such a fortune. 4. As a girl, Ola gave up her education to help support her family. She took care of her relatives when they were ill. **B.** People at her bank helped Ola invest her savings. They also figured out a plan to look after her when she could no longer work. They even helped her get an air conditioner. Ola only used it when visitors came to her house.

Page 71 **B.** 1. She had to overcome poverty, the illness of her relatives, and lack of education. 2. She had lived a hard life but was giving away her savings to help others and give them a chance for a better life. 3. She won respect, admiration, rewards, and love.

Page 72 **A.** 1. Oseola McCarty and her family were poor so they were probably unhappy. 2. The women in Ola's family took in laundry because it was most likely the only thing they could do. 3. Ola saved money instead of spending it, so she probably didn't care for material things. 4. Ola lived a quiet life because she didn't care about people. 5. *Oseola McCarty's Simple Wisdom for Rich Living* was published in 1996 and is the best book of its kind. **B.** 1. He thought she was unselfish and sensitive to others. 2. She thought it was important. 3. Answers may vary, but students might say that the writer shows admiration and respect.